D1607123

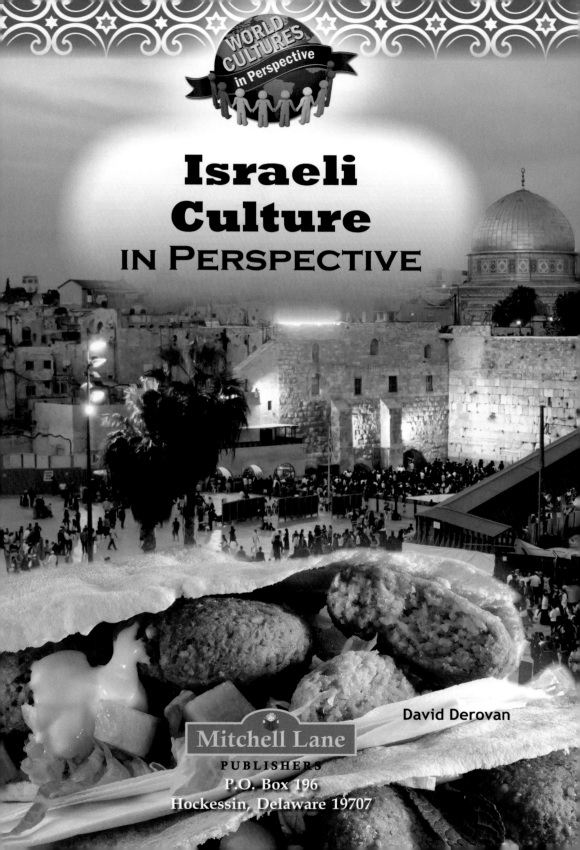

WORLD CULTURES in Perspective

Israeli
Culture
IN PERSPECTIVE

David Derovan

Mitchell Lane
PUBLISHERS
P.O. Box 196
Hockessin, Delaware 19707

Brazilian Cultures IN PERSPECTIVE

Caribbean Cultures IN PERSPECTIVE

East Asian Cultures IN PERSPECTIVE

Islamic Culture IN PERSPECTIVE

Israeli Culture IN PERSPECTIVE

Louisiana Cajun & Creole Cultures
IN PERSPECTIVE

Native Alaskan Cultures IN PERSPECTIVE

North African Cultures IN PERSPECTIVE

Polynesian Cultures IN PERSPECTIVE

Southeast Asian Cultures IN PERSPECTIVE

Mitchell Lane
PUBLISHERS

Printing   1   2   3   4   5   6   7   8   9

Library of Congress Cataloging-in-Publication Data
Derovan, David Jay.
  Israeli culture in perspective / by David Derovan.
        p. cm — (World cultures in perspective)
  Summary: "This book explores the cultures across Israel. Learn about the people, lifestyles, food, politics, music, dance, religion, language, arts, architecture, education, sports and so on, and how they affect the culture of the Israel"—Provided by publisher.
  Includes bibliographical references and index.
  ISBN 978-1-61228-566-5 (library bound)
  1. Israel—Social life and customs—Juvenile literature. 2. Israelis—Juvenile literature. 3. National characteristics, Israeli—Juvenile literature. I. Title.
  DS112.D38 2014
  956.94—dc23
                                                                    2014009363

eBook ISBN: 9781612286051

PUBLISHER'S NOTE: The fictionalized narrative used in portions of this book are an aid to comprehension. It is subject to interpretation and might not be indicative of every child's life. It is representative of some children and is based on research the author believes to be accurate. Documentation of such research is contained on pp. 60–61.

The Internet sites referenced herein were active as of the publication date. Due to the fleeting nature of some web sites, we cannot guarantee they will all be active when you are reading this book.

To reflect current usage, we have chosen to use the secular era designations BCE ("before the common era") and CE ("of the common era") instead of the traditional designations BC ("before Christ") and AD (*anno Domini,* "in the year of the Lord").

PBP

CONTENTS

INTRODUCTION
An Ancient Culture in Modern Times

What Is Culture?
Before we discuss Israeli culture, we must define the word culture. The *Concise Oxford English Dictionary* describes culture as behavior, arts, beliefs, and other products of human work and thought that are passed from one generation to another.[1] In other words, culture is what people do and the things they create, especially over time.

Israel has one dominant, overall culture that touches every Israeli's life. This general culture includes things like listening to the radio, involvement in politics, reading newspapers, or snacking on falafel or pizza. At the same time, Israel is home to many cultures because people have come to live in Israel from all over the world. For more than one hundred years, more and more people of all kinds have moved to Israel. A short review of the history of Israel will help us understand where these different people came from.

The Historical Basis of Israeli Culture
The land of Israel has been the homeland of the Jewish people since the time of the Bible, for over three thousand years. Even when other nations conquered the land and exiled the Jews, there were always Jews living in Israel.[2]

In the mid-1800s, only a handful of Jews lived in Israel. Then everything changed. Growing anti-Semitism in Russia and Eastern Europe caused numerous Jews to move to Israel in the 1880s and 1890s.[3] This was known as the First Aliyah, or ascent, to Israel. The Second Aliyah began in 1903 after a horrible anti-Jewish riot in the city of Kishinev, Russia.[4]

In the 1930s and 1940s, Nazi Germans killed and tortured Jews in an attempt to destroy the entire Jewish population. This mass murder, called the Holocaust, was one of the causes of World War II (1939–1945). During this time, many Jews succeeded in migrating to Israel.[5]

By 1948, when the modern State of Israel was established, the Jewish population of Israel had grown substantially. The Arab population also grew during the first half of the twentieth century. As more Jews arrived, so did the Arabs, who were interested in expanding their businesses.[6]

After 1948, over seven hundred thousand Jews arrived from all over North Africa and the Middle East. Like the European Jews before them, these Jews also came because of persecution.[7] Over time, the two large groups of Jews from Eastern Europe and the Middle East were joined by Americans, Canadians, British, South Americans, South Africans, more Russians, Ethiopians, and others. Each group brought its own unique culture.

Many aspects of these different cultures have combined to create contemporary Israeli culture. However, these groups still retain many aspects of their own cultural identities.

We will explore both the common elements that make up general Israeli culture and individual Israeli cultures with the help of a group of fourteen-year-old Israelis named Nadav, Shmulik, Ziva, Ori, and Yityish.

So let's meet them!

Israeli Culture in a Nutshell

Official Name: State of Israel
Form of Government: parliamentary democracy
Capital: Jerusalem
Area: 22,072 square kilometers (8,522 square miles), slightly larger than New Jersey
Official Languages: Hebrew, Arabic
Currency: Israeli new shekel
Population:
- 8.018 million people on the eve of Israel's sixty-fifth Independence Day (2013)
- At the time of the establishment of the state, it numbered 806,000 residents.
- The Jewish population: 6.042 million (75.3% of the population)
- The Arab population: 1.658 million (20.7%)
- Non-Arab Christians, members of other religions, and others: 318,000 (4.0%)
- At the end of 2011, over 70% of the total Jewish population were *sabras*—born in Israel—compared with only 35% native-born in 1948.
- In 1948, Tel Aviv-Yafo was the only city with more than one hundred thousand residents.
- Today, fourteen cities number more than one hundred thousand residents, of which six number more than two hundred thousand residents: Jerusalem, Tel Aviv-Yafo, Haifa, Rishon LeZiyyon, Ashdod, and Petah Tikva.[8]

Cultural Institutions:
- 231 museums of every kind[9]
- theater companies
- an opera company
- numerous dance companies and groups
- music festivals
- film festivals[10]

Tel Aviv Museum of Art

- "Hebrew Book Week"—ten days of discounted books offered by dozens of publishers in five major locations in the biggest cities and around the country[11]

CHAPTER ONE
A Strange Meeting

It all began in a Jerusalem health clinic waiting room. The nurse called out the last name of the next person to get the annual flu shot, "Rabinowitz!" Three young people got up. Each one said, "I'm Rabinowitz." Then, they looked at each other: two boys and a girl with the same last name who obviously did not know each other, but lived in the same neighborhood. How strange! Then, a fourth young man stood up and said, "I'm also a Rabinowitz . . . at least that used to be our family name."

"How can we all be Rabinowitzes if we are not related?" asked the fair-haired young man.

"Maybe we *are* related," countered the young lady.

"I have an idea. Let's meet after we get our shots and talk about this," suggested the third Rabinowitz.

"Okay," they all replied. And that's what they did.

An hour later, in a café around the corner, five fourteen-year-olds sat at a table in awkward silence. "So, who are you?" asked the young lady.

"I am Shmulik Rabinowitz," began the young fellow who was wearing a cap called a *kippah* and had short, curled sidelocks hanging near his ears. "I live just a short walk away and attend *yeshiva*, religious school, here in the neighborhood."

"My name is Nadav," said the boy with the dirty blond hair and blue eyes. "I also live nearby and go to school here, but I'm not religious like Shmulik."

The third boy had jet black hair and an olive complexion. He smiled and announced, "I'm here because my great-grandfather changed his family name from Rabinowitz to Ben-Rabi when he moved to Morocco. So, I'm also a Rabinowitz. Oh, and my name is Ori. We are a traditional family. We observe the Sabbath, but we are not strictly religious."

"I guess that leaves me," said the girl. "I am Ziva Rabinowitz and I also live and go to school here. And this is my friend Yityish Abtow," pointing to the young black girl sitting beside her. "In case you haven't guessed," Ziva said with a big smile, "she is Ethiopian and she's not a Rabinowitz!" Everyone, including Yityish, laughed. "So, are we related somehow?" asked Ziva.

Ori answered, "We could be. But we are so different from one another."

"Yes and no," said Nadav. "We look different. We are religiously different, but we are all Israelis who are in eighth grade, living in the same neighborhood of Jerusalem. There are probably many things that we and our families have in common."

"We all listen to music," said Shmulik. "Although I think that our tastes are different."

"Nevertheless, we all love music, just as all Israelis love music," added Ori. "In fact, for a small country, we have many major orchestras, jazz bands, and pop and rock groups. There are more than a half a dozen radio stations that all day long play Israeli music and music from around the world.[1] Israel has a large recording industry that puts out albums with every kind of music from classical to rock and pop to ethnic and religious music."

"Don't forget all of the music festivals. Then there are theater festivals, art museums and art galleries, and the annual art festivals," said Yityish.[2]

"And books," Ziva said with a dreamy smile. "Every year, Israel publishes more than six thousand books of every kind![3] I just love Book Week every June. It's so much fun to wander up and down all the aisles between the stalls and see so many different kinds of books on every topic imaginable—all in Hebrew!"[4]

"This is what my mother calls culture!" announced Nadav. "Israelis live in a very rich cultural environment, she says."

After a moment of silence, Nadav spoke again, "There are other things we have in common as Israelis. After high school, we serve in the army. Well, at least most of us do, except some groups like the *haredim* (the ultra-religious Israelis)."

"Not true," said Shmulik, blushing. "Yes, for a very long time haredi men did not serve, but that's changing. Now there is a special unit just for very religious men and more and more of them are serving in the IDF (the Israel Defense Forces)." After catching his breath, Shmulik quickly changed the subject, "Don't forget that all Israelis love electronic gadgets, especially cell phones!"

"And sports!" called out Ori. "I have a favorite soccer team, a favorite basketball team, a favorite handball team, a favorite volleyball team, and . . ."

"OK," said Ziva, "we get the message. Yes, as Israelis, we love sports, too."

"You cannot forget the Internet. I'm sure we all use the Internet, even Shmulik, right?" added Yityish. Everyone turned to look at Shmulik who was a bit embarrassed by the question.

"We do not have an Internet connection on our home computer," he admitted. "As very religious Jews, our family feels it could be a bad influence on our behavior." His face got a bit redder and then he added with a sheepish smile, "But I do go to a friend's house to use the Internet on his computer."

"See, I was right," announced Yityish. "Now that we have established that we all take part in the common Israeli culture, I am interested to find out two things. The first is what makes each of you Rabinowitzes different and second, how you are all related."

The sport of basketball has many Israeli fans. Here, Devin Smith of the Maccabi Tel Aviv team scores in a February 2014 playoff game against Galatasaray Istanbul.

After a moment's thought, Ziva proposed that they meet each day during the following week in a different home and try to answer Yityish's questions. Everyone agreed. So, they exchanged addresses and phone numbers and planned to meet first at Nadav's house.

Israeli soldiers drive a Merkava battle
tank, designed and built in Israel.

The IDF: The Israel Defense Forces

The IDF is one of the most sophisticated and successful armies in the world, despite its small size.[5] Since Israel is a long, narrow country, the IDF is divided into three major command groups: Northern, Central, and Southern Commands. There is also a Home Front Command in charge of protecting civilians during wartime.[6]

In addition, the IDF has an air force, a navy, and ground troops. The ground troops are divided up into a number of brigades (very large groups) that include the paratroopers, armor corps (tanks), artillery corps, and various special forces.

The IDF was established on May 31, 1948, just after the State of Israel was founded. It was immediately involved in the Israeli War of Independence from May 1948 until July 1949, when Israel defeated the combined armies of five Arab countries. Since then the IDF has fought in six major wars: In 1956, Israel launched the Sinai Campaign to protect itself from Egyptian attacks. On the morning of June 5, 1967, Israel once again attacked Egypt in self-defense. In six short days, the IDF defeated the armies of Egypt, Jordan, and Syria. In 1973, Egypt and Syria attacked Israel, but were defeated again. The IDF has also fought in Lebanon twice, in 1982 and 2006. Most recently, in 2008 and 2009 Israel fought in the three-week Gaza War. This conflict came in response to rockets being fired into Israel by Palestinians in the Gaza Strip.[7]

Nadav

Nadav Rabinowitz lived with his family on the tenth floor of a modern apartment building. The furnishings were all very modern and tasteful. Similar to most Israeli apartments, the rooms were not very large, but were comfortable.

All the young Rabinowitzes and Yityish sat around the dining room table. Nadav's mother had put out beverages, a package of cookies, and a bowl of fruit. She left the cookies in their package so Shmulik and the others could see that the snack was kosher. Shmulik muttered a thank you to Nadav and ate a cookie.

"I want you to understand who I am and what my family's culture is like. So, I must begin with a bit of family history," said Nadav. "I am a fifth-generation Israeli. My great-great-great-grandfather, Moshe Rabinowitz came to Israel in 1882 with his wife Hanna."

"That's during the First Aliyah," commented Ziva.

"What is the First Aliyah?" asked Yityish.

Nadav answered, "The first big wave of European Jews returning to the land of Israel is called the First Aliyah, or ascent to Israel. It took place during the 1880s and 1890s. These people were the ones who started farms in northern Israel."[1]

"The region was called the Galilee region," continued Ori.

"Jews of Central or Eastern European origin are called Ashkenazic Jews," said Nadav. "European Jewish history goes back over two thousand years, to the time of the Second Temple in Jerusalem. However, the Jews of Eastern Europe experienced many pogroms . . . "

Again Yityish interrupted, "Excuse me for asking another question—what is a pogrom?"

Nadav responded, "A pogrom is a riot led by anti-Semites for the purpose of murdering Jews and destroying their property. Moshe Rabinowitz and his wife came to Israel as pogroms were becoming common across Russia. They settled in Jerusalem.

"Since then, my family lived on a kibbutz, in the town of Petah Tikva and in Tel Aviv before coming back to Jerusalem. Like so many other Ashkenazic families, we drifted away from religious observance and became active in the leading political parties . . ."

"Which were socialist and Ashkenazic," commented Ziva.

After a momentary pause, Yityish challenged Nadav, "So what makes you and your Ashkenazic family unique?"

"Oddly enough," answered Nadav, "the Holocaust makes us unique. On my father's side, my great-grandfather fought in the Jewish Brigade for the British during World War II.[2] On my mother's side, most of her family that remained in Europe was murdered by the Nazis during the war. The scars caused by the Holocaust never seem to go away. They are passed on from generation to generation."

"Can I ask Yityish's question again?" asked Shmulik. "We all have studied about the Holocaust, because it is a very important landmark in modern Jewish history. And as Israelis, every year we commemorate together—everyone, not just Ashkenazic Jews—the tragedy of the Holocaust.[3] However, I want to ask Yityish's question about you, Nadav, and your family. What makes Nadav Rabinowitz unique as an Ashkenazic Jew?"

Nadav sat silently for a minute or two and then answered Shmulik. "I think the best way to say it is that my father Shahar,

In this illustration of an 1880s Russian pogrom, Jews are attacked as the police look on.

my mother Ya'el, my brother Ilan, my sister Mara, and I live as Ashkenazic Israelis. We live the Ashkenazic Israeli way of life. For instance, breakfast is a salad of diced cucumbers and tomatoes with a bit of olive oil sprinkled on top, along with bread and white cheese spread. Lunch is a three-course meat meal, which starts with soup, then chicken and potatoes and veggies, and ends with compote, fruit cooked in heavy syrup. Dinner is eaten late, around

Early settlers in Palestine–Israel tending their garden in 1900.

eight o'clock, and is similar to breakfast, except that it includes quiche or scrambled eggs.[4]

"On vacation days, my parents still take the traditional afternoon nap between two and four o'clock. On Saturdays, we love to hike in the hills around Jerusalem or we travel to the beach in Tel Aviv or Ashkelon during the summer months."

"That's it?" asked Ori in a surprised tone.

"Oh, there's more. We read the newspaper every day. On Friday, my father brings home more than one weekend newspaper. And then there are all the other things we have in common that we talked about the other day."

Again, Yityish jumped in, "So, what makes you different from the Ashkenazic Jews of previous generations?"

Nadav smiled broadly. "I'm happy Ziva brought you along. Good question! Unlike my grandparents, who are totally secular and non-religious, we belong to the group of secular Israelis who are slowly returning to our Jewish roots, as my mother loves to say.[5] We observe the basic kosher laws at home. On Passover, we have a family *seder*. On Rosh Hashanah and Yom Kippur, we pray in the synagogue. And my parents attend classes about Judaism and study classic Jewish texts."

The young people looked at Nadav and all together said, "Thank you!"

"Would you like to see some photos of the 'olden' days?"

"Sure!" they answered and Nadav stood to lead them into the living room.

"Wait," said Ziva. "Where are we meeting tomorrow?"

"How about my house?" suggested Shmulik.

The ceiling of the Hall of Names in the Holocaust History Museum at Yad Vashem in Jerusalem. The ceiling is a thirty-foot-high cone where six hundred photographs are displayed, representing just a fraction of the six million Jewish men, women, and children murdered by the Nazis in Europe during World War II (1939–1945).

The Kibbutz

The Hebrew word kibbutz means "group." The kibbutz is a uniquely Israeli community. It is based on joint ownership of property and wealth and provides for every kibbutz member, young and old. The first kibbutzim (plural of kibbutz) were established in northern Israel in the 1910s and 1920s. Today, there are over 270 kibbutzim in Israel. Many of the earliest kibbutzim were devoted exclusively to agriculture. However, today, kibbutz members have careers of all kinds outside of the kibbutz, and the majority of kibbutzim have factories as well.[6]

Over time, things have changed on many of the kibbutzim. For many years, all children slept in supervised dormitories. Nowadays, children sleep at home. Until recently, kibbutz members ate all of their meals together in the dining room. Today, some kibbutzim have closed the dining room because more and more families eat together.

The kibbutzim have been an important part of Israeli history. Many of the IDF's commanders and officers came from the kibbutzim, along with many of Israel's political leaders.

CHAPTER THREE
Shmulik

Shmulik Rabinowitz and his family lived in the ground floor apartment of a four-story building. As Shmulik led them on a tour of his home, the other Rabinowitzes and Yityish noticed that there were many bedrooms, each smaller than the bedrooms in Nadav's home. The kitchen was a good size and they could see a backyard through the kitchen window. However, the dining room and living room area—one big room—was filled from end to end with a large table surrounded by chairs, while the walls were lined with bookcases overflowing with books.

"I counted nine beds!" exclaimed Yityish as everyone sat down at one end of the long table.

"That's because we have seven children," said Shmulik's mother Yentel, who had suddenly appeared in the doorway to the kitchen. Yentel wore a scarf on her head that prevented anyone from seeing her hair. The young people noted that this was a common practice of haredi wives. "Shmulik is our youngest," she added and then disappeared down the hall carrying her load of clean laundry.

A minute or two later, Shmulik's mother placed a package of cookies on the table along with a bowl of fruit and drinks. Nadav held up the package of cookies and looked at Shmulik. "Yes, we like the same kind of cookies, Nadav," smiled Shmulik. "Another thing we have in common."

Shmulik began, "I want to start with two things. The first is: Does anyone know what the name 'Rabinowitz' means?"

They all shook their heads no.

"It means," continued Shmulik, "son of a rabbi. In fact, like Nadav's family, my siblings and I are also fifth-generation Israelis, except that we have always lived in Jerusalem. And a number of my ancestors were indeed rabbis."

"Is your father a rabbi?" asked Nadav.

"No," replied Shmulik. "He is a businessman."

"What's the second thing you wanted to tell us?" asked Ori.

"I wanted to say that I found what Nadav told us very interesting," said Shmulik. "Actually, I learned something very important from Nadav. From his description of Ashkenazic Israeli culture you see that culture is really a combination of two things: It is the continuation of a tradition, and it is the change of those traditions over time. Nadav's family still does so many things that his grandparents and great-grandparents did, but they are also doing new things, different things.

"The same is true about my family. My family has always been strictly religious, haredi. Our family's cultural life is defined by Jewish religious culture. We observe the Torah's commandments very carefully, and we spend many long hours and years studying Torah. All the books you see on the shelves around us are not just read. They are studied. We learn how to behave, how to eat kosher food, how to observe the Sabbath, and so much more from them. On the other hand, our culture is changing."

"Do you mean the use of computers and cell phones and modern appliances?" asked Ziva. "I saw more than one computer in the different bedrooms."

Shmulik thought for a minute and then answered, "That is only a small part of it. Everyone in Israel has cell phones and computers

Three haredi Jewish women talking on the street in the Mea Shearim neighborhood of Jerusalem, Israel.

and food processors, even haredim. What I'm talking about is a deeper change."

Nadav cut in, "You are talking about going to the army, aren't you?"

"Yes," agreed Shmulik. "That is one of the big changes that are just starting to happen. The other change is that in the last few years, haredi Jews, who would never have thought of getting a degree, are now studying in colleges and universities. Our community realizes that good jobs require general knowledge and training."

"Well," started Yityish and everyone turned to look at their wise Ethiopian friend, "it seems to me as if you are going through a process of discovering how to live a very religious Jewish lifestyle and culture while becoming part of the modern world."

"Yes," said Shmulik. "You have to understand that for the last two generations, haredi men in Israel studied full-time in yeshiva while the women worked to support them. They also received money from the yeshiva. Today, there is less money because the government has reduced the payments it gives to the yeshivot. So, more and more men are going to work."

"So, you are an Ashkenazic Jew like Nadav, whose family has been in Israel for five generations like Nadav's family, but your experience and the changes you are going through are so different!" exclaimed Ori. "So what I want to know is what kinds of food you eat?"

The laughter signaled that the serious conversation was over.

"Well, Ori, when is the last time you had *cholent*?" asked Shmulik with a smile.

"You can't fool me," said Ori. "My mother cooks cholent, but we call it *hamin*."[1]

"OK, you both lost me!" said Yityish. "What is cholent? And what is hamin?"

"Please let me explain," offered Ziva. "Cholent and hamin are both names for a large stew. A pot is filled with chunks of meat, potatoes, vegetables, beans, and barley—and I bet Ori's mother also puts in chickpeas and hard-boiled eggs—and the cooking begins before sundown on Friday afternoon. Then the pot is left to simmer on the stove overnight. It is removed from the stove at lunchtime. The result is a delicious, hot meal.

"We cook it that way for a reason. According to the Torah, among the activities that cannot be performed on the Sabbath— from sundown Friday to after dark on Saturday—is cooking. To have a hot meal for lunch on the Sabbath, we make cholent and Ori's mother makes hamin."

The conversation about food continued until it was time to go. The next day was Ori's turn to host the group.

The Yeshiva

In the Hebrew Bible, God urges the Jewish people to teach their children about Judaism. As a result, Jews have been studying Torah, the Bible, and other religious books, for over 2,500 years. The school where this study takes place for young people and adults is called a yeshiva, literally, "a place of sitting" in Hebrew. The very first yeshiva was established over two thousand years ago in the land of Israel.

Today, the yeshiva style of study is based on such schools that existed in Central and Eastern Europe for the last one thousand years.

Studying Talmud in a yeshiva.

In the past, only the best students continued to study in the yeshiva after the age of thirteen.[2] Today, there are more Jews studying in yeshivot for more years than at any time before in Jewish history.[3]

In Israel, haredi and religious-national men study in yeshivot. Women study in similar schools called seminaries or *midrashot*. Jewish studies are also taught in all seven of Israel's universities and in many of its colleges. In addition, even Israelis who are not religious are studying Torah in greater numbers.

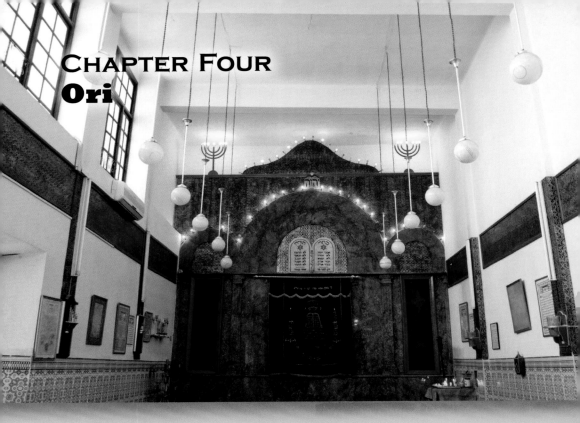

CHAPTER FOUR
Ori

When Ori opened the door to his apartment to greet Yityish and his Rabinowitz guests, they were greeted with the delicious smell of cooking. As they gathered around the dining room table, Ori's mother Sima came in from the kitchen to greet them.

"What are you cooking?" asked Ziva, expressing what everyone was thinking. "It smells wonderful!"

"Oh, you'll find out later," answered Sima, "because you are all staying for lunch."

"OK!" "All right!" "Sure!" they all answered enthusiastically.

"Here is something to eat in the meantime," said Sima as she placed a platter piled with small pastries on the table.

As his mother returned to the kitchen, Ori said, "Already you can see a big part of my Sephardic culture. We insist on feeding our guests. By the way, the pastries are called *ma'amoulim*, rolled dough filled with either dates and nuts or chocolate. You'll find some of each on the platter my mother brought in."

All talking stopped because everyone was busy sampling the sweet pastries.

"So, Ori," began Yityish, "tell us how an Ashkenazic Rabinowitz can become a Sephardic Jew."

"Well," answered Ori with a smile, "I spoke with my father and learned some very interesting things about my family that I didn't know before. Nadav, you and I are cousins!"

Nadav's face showed shock and pleasure all at the same time. "Wow!" he exclaimed.

"Let me explain," continued Ori. "Back in 1915, my great-great-grandfather David Rabinowitz married Miriam Schloss on a kibbutz in the Galilee. They had two sons. The younger son, Shimon, was born in 1918 and he was Nadav's great-grandfather. The older son, Reuben, was born in 1917. In 1937, he moved to Casablanca, Morocco, because he was offered a job there. In 1945, he married Mazal Aflalo. Since he was living and working in a Sephardic community for a long time and was now marrying into the community, he changed his family name to Ben-Rabi, which is a Hebrew translation of Rabinowitz, meaning son of a rabbi. He also adopted Moroccan Jewish customs. So, here I am three generations later, a Sephardic Jew with Ashkenazic roots!"

"So when did your family come back to Israel?" asked Shmulik.

"In the 1950s and 1960s, there was a mass aliyah, immigration, of Moroccan Jews to Israel.[1] My grandfather Aharon and his new wife Susie were among them," explained Ori.

"But there are so many kinds of Sephardic Jews!" said Yityish.

Ori smiled and answered, "It is confusing, even for me! Sephardic refers to Jews whose origins can be traced to Spain, called Sepharad, in Hebrew. In the late 1400s in Spain, the Christians demanded that the Jews convert to Christianity. Those Jews who refused to convert were forced to leave Spain.[2] Most of them settled in North Africa and the Middle East. All of these communities, together with the Jews who already lived in such places as Iraq and Syria and Yemen, are lumped together in the category called Sephardic. Nevertheless, each community, from each different country, has a unique culture all of its own."

"What makes them different from one another?" asked Nadav.

"Each community has a slightly different prayer book. The traditional foods are different. They speak different dialects of Arabic. Their traditional clothes are not the same. These things belong to the first part of culture mentioned by Nadav and Shmulik," said Ori.

"It seems to me that you are not exactly like your Moroccan great-grandfather, are you, Ori?" asked Ziva.

"No," replied Ori. "That is the second part of culture. Many Sephardic Israelis have changed."

"How?" asked Ziva again.

"First of all, many of us are no longer as religiously observant as our ancestors. My family has a strictly kosher kitchen and we attend Sabbath synagogue services on Friday night and Saturday morning. However, we use the telephone and sometimes go for a ride in our car on the Sabbath, which are things Shmulik's family would never do."[3]

"But so much of our common Israeli experience is Sephardic!" said Yityish enthusiastically.

A Jewish family in Morocco, 1880s

"That is another big change," said Ori. "For so many years, Sephardic culture in Israel was sort of hidden. You didn't hear Sephardic music on the radio and Sephardic restaurants served Ashkenazic food.[4] But all that has changed. Now, there are many Sephardic restaurants serving traditional Sephardic food and Sephardic music is everywhere.

"When we first came from all over the Middle East and North Africa to Israel in the 1960s, the majority, Ashkenazic Israelis, thought we were ignorant, uncultured people.[5] Over time, we became successful in business, and attended colleges and universities like the Ashkenazic Israelis and, most important of all, many Ashkenazic Jews married Sephardic Jews. The result is that Sephardic culture—music, dance, food, clothing, speech patterns—are now basic parts of overall Israeli culture."[6]

"OK, enough serious talk," announced Sima. "Now, it's time for lunch."

All the young people got up to help set the table and bring out the food. Sima had prepared spicy fish filets; *mujadra*, rice with lentils; *shu'it*, yellow beans in sauce; and *kubbeh*, deep-fried, oblong balls of bulgur (grain) filled with a mixture of diced onions and spicy chopped lamb.

"What a feast!" "Delicious!" "Mmmm!" they exclaimed.

At the end of the meal, Ziva announced, "Tomorrow, we'll meet at my house and I have some surprises for all of you!"

Moroccan Jews arriving in Israel by boat, 1962.

The Spanish Inquisition

Until 1492, Spain had the largest Jewish population in Europe.[7] After the Christians chased the Muslims out of southern Spain, they began to demand that the Jews convert to Christianity. Many of the Jews who converted continued to observe their Judaism in secret. These people were called *marranos*, which means "pigs" in Spanish. To test the sincerity of the Jewish converts, in 1478, King Ferdinand and Queen Isabella established the Inquisition, special courts where the Jewish converts were put on trial.[8]

Many Jews died during the Inquisition, and others left Spain. Some of these Jews moved to other European countries such as Italy, but the majority resettled throughout North Africa and the Middle East.

Today, many Spanish families still observe certain Jewish customs. They are often surprised to discover that their ancestors were marranos.

Jews on trial in Madrid during the Spanish Inquisition.

CHAPTER FIVE
Ziva

Western Wall, 1870s

Ziva lived in a single-family one-story house on a street lined with trees, which was rare in most Jerusalem neighborhoods. The other Rabinowitzes and Yityish sat around the dining room table munching on cookies and fruit as Ziva began her story.

"Yesterday, I mentioned that I have some surprises for everyone, but they will have to wait until the end of our meeting, except for one. My Rabinowitz great-great-grandfather was born in Israel in 1890, but he moved to America when he was eighteen. So, my grandfather was born in the United States and came to Israel after high school. He studied in a yeshiva in Jerusalem and then he stayed in Israel. He fought in the famous 1967 Six-Day War.[1] As a result, I still have many relatives living in the United States. However, it may come as a bigger surprise that my father is a career officer in the IDF. He is a colonel in military intelligence."

"Why should that be a surprise," said Nadav with a shrug. "We all know that more and more Israeli army officers are religious. You can identify them by the knitted kippah they wear."

Israeli soldiers celebrating Israel's victory in the 1967 Six-Day War.

"So how does your American background affect your family's culture?" asked Ori.

"It affects us in many ways," answered Ziva. "First, is the fact that my parents, my brothers, my sister, and I all speak English. Second, our family culture is relatively new. Third, we are religious nationalists. This means that we are also religious—not like Ori's family—more like Shmulik's family, but all the men work for a living after studying in yeshiva for a few years. They also serve in the army, while the girls do national service, working in hospitals and schools. Most religious nationalists also have college or university degrees."

"Is being a religious nationalist like being a Zionist?" asked Shmulik.

"Yes, it means that we are firm believers in the Zionist dream of the return of the entire Jewish people to the land of Israel. We support the State of Israel and participate fully in Israeli society, just like Nadav and Ori's families," answered Ziva.

Shmulik interrupted Ziva, "Haredi Israelis are also Zionists! We wouldn't live anywhere else but in Israel. However, our political ideas are very different."

"Sorry, Shmulik," said Ziva. "I certainly did not mean to insult haredim. I was just trying to explain about our family."

"No problem," replied Shmulik.

"I guess my point is this," continued Ziva. "Our culture is more of a combination of new things than a continuation of older traditions. Yes, the Jewish religion provides us with a strong basis, but beyond that we are truly modern people and we have forged our own new Israeli culture. It includes our schools, where the students study religious texts along with science, literature, and history. We have our own political parties, and we are dedicated to the State of Israel and to serving in the army. In addition, our lives are filled with everything Israel has to offer culturally, from different ethnic foods and all kinds of music to every form of entertainment and art."[2]

Somewhat out of breath, Ziva was pleased that Yityish had a comment to make.

"It seems to me," she said, "that your family culture is a combination of Nadav's, Shmulik's, and Ori's. Your family has adopted large chunks of all the major cultures in Israel."

"Yes," said Ziva.

"So, what do you eat that's different?" asked Ori with his big smile.

"Oh, Ori, you're always interested in food!" exclaimed Shmulik.

"I think it's a good question," said Nadav. "What makes the food in this Rabinowitz household different?"

"I guess you can say that we eat what all of you eat. However, my mother loves to try new recipes, especially her own new ones," was Ziva's reply.

"Can you give us an example?" asked Yityish.

"Have any of you ever had honey-garlic chicken?" Ziva inquired. They all said, "No."

Higher education is important to many religious nationalists. Here, a young Israeli woman studies at a library at the Hebrew University in Jerusalem.

"Well, it's great!" said Ziva enthusiastically.

"So?" they all said together.

"OK," she continued. "It's really easy to make. Take a roasting pan and line the bottom with a half-centimeter of water and sliced onions. Arrange pieces of chicken in the pan. Then cover all the pieces completely with garlic powder. On top of that drip honey over everything. Then bake it until the chicken is soft."

"Mmm," said Ori. "I'm getting hungry!"

"What about the other surprises?" Nadav asked.

"Good that you reminded me," said Ziva. "Here is surprise number one: I have been talking with all of your parents and based on what they told me I created a family tree. So, guess what?"

"Don't tell me," said Shmulik. "We are all related!"

"Yes!" shouted Ziva. "Yes! Each of our families can be traced back six generations to Moshe and Hanna Rabinowitz, who came to Israel in 1882. Moshe and Hanna had three sons. The oldest, Sholom, was my great-great-grandfather. The middle son, Isaac, was Shmulik's great-great-grandfather, and the youngest, David, was Nadav and Ori's great-great-grandfather. So, we are all cousins!"

"Amazing!" "Wow" "How cool!" came the responses.

"And I would like to have your agreement," continued Ziva, "in declaring Yityish an honorary member of the extended Rabinowitz family."

"Yes!" they all shouted together. Yityish beamed with joy.

"Now, for the next surprise: Apparently, Moshe and Hanna's apartment that they lived in when they arrived from Europe still exists." Ziva stopped to allow the news to sink in while everyone's eyes lit up.

"Tomorrow, we will gather at Yityish's house to learn about Ethiopian Israeli culture, but next week, my father is going to accompany us to the Old City section of Jerusalem so we can find the apartment," announced Ziva.

"Wow!" said Shmulik. "I think I speak for everyone when I say that cousin Ziva has really surprised us all!"

Aliyah from North America

Among all of the Jewish organizations in North America, many are Zionist, dedicated to Israel. For over a hundred years, North American Jews have given very generously to Israel and to Israeli institutions. Indeed, millions of dollars are raised for Israel every year in North America.

However, there have never been great waves of North American aliyah to Israel. One of the reasons is that the Israeli lifestyle is so different. Nevertheless, this situation is beginning to change. In 2002, a new organization devoted to North American aliyah—called Nefesh B'Nefesh—was established. The group's efforts have been successful and North Americans are coming in ever greater numbers to live in Israel.

However, even with the two-thousand-plus North American Jews who come every year,[3] those numbers are just a drop in the bucket when compared to the 5.8 million Jews who live in North America.[4] Today, over fifty thousand North American Jews call Israel home.[5]

Friday evening Sabbath services at the Sixth & I synagogue in downtown Washington, DC.

CHAPTER SIX
Yityish

The apartment building where Yityish lived with her family was just like many of the others. The Abtow family lived on the third floor. The Rabinowitzes gathered around the dining room table while Yityish brought in drinks and cookies.

As they filled their mouths with cookies, Yityish began. "In general, my story is the same as yours. My family came to Israel from far away. We brought our traditional culture with us and we are experiencing many changes. However, the details are very different. Your family came to Israel from Europe almost 130 years ago. We came just 30 years ago. You continued your age-old Jewish religious traditions; we had to change our traditions drastically. Your family has been part of modern life. Most Ethiopian Jews came to Israel from small villages where there was no electricity or running water."[1]

The young Rabinowitzes listened intently.

"But even though there were many difficult changes, our family wouldn't want to be anywhere else. We have waited thousands of years to return to the land of Israel and to Jerusalem and now we are finally here!" Yityish smiled broadly.

Ori asked, "So, when did your family come to Israel?"

"We came," continued Yityish, "during Operation Moses in 1985. My parents were young children who came with almost eight thousand others. They walked from Ethiopia to Sudan. My grandmother died along the way. Ever since, Ethiopian Jews have come to Israel. The biggest group came on Operation Solomon. On May 24, 1991, the State of Israel sent thirty-three airplanes, many of them with the seats removed so more people could fit into the planes. Over fourteen thousand people boarded the planes. This was the largest airlift of people in so little time."[2]

"We learned in class," said Ziva, "that when one of the pilots was asked why they took the seats out, he answered that this way no one was going to be left behind."

Israeli soldiers assist newly arrived Ethiopian Jews in Israel, May 25, 1991.

Shmulik commented, "I saw in the *Guinness Book of World Records* that one plane had over one thousand people in it! The most passengers ever to fly in one plane together!"[3]

"Please tell us about how you have changed culturally," said Nadav.

"Most Ethiopian Jews lived in villages in the mountains," started Yityish. "The houses were made of mud and wood.[4] My family lived near streams so they had water. There was no electricity for refrigerators, so they cooked fresh food every day. Some fathers were sheep or cattle herders. Some were craftsmen. The mothers were responsible for the home and the children. Everyone knew their place. The community looked up to the religious leader, called a *kes*. Then there were the heads of each extended family. The fathers of individual families were next in line. The children were on the lowest rung of the society ladder.[5] In Ethiopia, children are taught not to look their elders directly in the eye because to do so is a sign of disrespect."[6]

"Let me guess," said Shmulik. "Here in Israel all of that has changed."

"Yes," replied Yityish. "We obviously do not live in mud houses anymore. In fact, most Ethiopian Jews never saw running water or used a gas stove and oven before coming to Israel. Ashkenazic and Sephardic Jews learned to read and write in Hebrew. It has always been part of your culture, but Ethiopian Jews did not learn Hebrew. Our religious writings are in Ge'ez, an ancient Ethiopian language. In addition, we have been removed from the Jewish mainstream for two thousand years. While Judaism has changed and developed over the years, we have continued to practice our faith the same way. Because of that, our kessim, religious leaders, don't have the same status as an Israeli rabbi. Weddings have to be performed by an Israeli rabbi to be legal in Israel."[7]

After catching her breath, Yityish continued, "Here, in Israel, the parents had to rely on their children, who quickly learned Hebrew and how to live in Israeli society. This has created many problems in Ethiopian Israeli families.

While the older generations of Ethiopian-Israelis have maintained many of their traditions, young people usually prefer to wear typical Israeli clothing and listen to popular music. Here, a group of Israeli-born teenagers enjoy the view of Jerusalem from a promenade.

"Ethiopian children and young adults are learning skills that our parents never had. As a young boy in Ethiopia, my father helped to herd the sheep. In Israel, he works in a dormitory kitchen. He helps serve the food and does the cleaning. My mother cleans houses. They speak enough Hebrew to get by, but do not read Hebrew. On the other hand, my brother is an officer in the army. My sister attends university and is studying business. I hope to go to medical school."[8]

"Aren't some things still the same?" asked Ori.

"Yes," answered Yityish. "We still celebrate the Sigd holiday, which always falls on the twenty-ninth day of the Hebrew month of Cheshvan. On this day, everyone dedicates himself to being a better person. When we were in Ethiopia, it was also a day for expressing our desire to return to Jerusalem. Now that we are in Israel, many of us travel to Jerusalem to celebrate. The first half of the day no one eats or drinks. Then there is a religious ceremony, which is followed by a big feast and dancing."

"I went to last year's Sigd festival with Yityish," said Ziva. "It was wonderful! Since 2008, Sigd is a national Israeli holiday!"[9]

"Did you mention food, Yityish?" asked Ori with one of his big smiles. Everyone laughed.

"Yes, Ori," smiled Yityish. "I did. So, let me tell you about food. This is one of the big changes we have gone through here in Israel. While we still eat mostly Ethiopian-style foods at home, we are slowly but surely learning to eat other foods. In fact, my parents love falafel, but only with a ton of the spicy sauce on top."

"Wow," said Shmulik. "That was amazing!" And everyone nodded their heads in agreement.

"Don't forget," said Ziva as they got up to leave. "Next week, we go to the Old City."

Celebrating the annual Ethiopian Sigd festival, Jerusalem 2013.

Traditional Ethiopian Food

The basis of the traditional Ethiopian meal is *injera*, a flat, thick bread. In Ethiopia, it was used instead of a fork and spoon. Either *wat*, a spicy stew containing meat and vegetables, is served on top of the injera, or the injera is used to scoop up everything from sauces to other foods. There are many different kinds of wat, each with its own name and its own recipe.[10]

Ethiopians only eat with their right hands. It is considered unclean to put food in your mouth with your left hand.

Since sugar was not widely available in Ethiopia until the 1960s, dessert was not a part of most traditional meals. While some Ethiopians have started to eat sweets at the end of their meals, they are more likely to end a large meal with a cup of strong coffee.

CHAPTER SEVEN
Mahmoud

Ziva's father drove the young people across town toward the Old City section of Jerusalem.

"Do you know some of the history of the Old City?" he asked.

"Yes," said Shmulik, "In 1538, the Ottoman emperor Suleiman the Magnificent constructed a wall around what was then the entire city of Jerusalem."

"The city was built on the foundations that were created when Jerusalem was ruled by the Romans. After they destroyed the Second Temple in 70 CE, they rebuilt the city and called it Aelia Capitolina. Today the Old City is divided into four parts or quarters," continued Nadav.

Ori added, "The thick stone walls rise up to fifteen meters (almost fifty feet) in height. There are thirty-four towers and eleven gates, but only seven of the gates are open."

"I think we know the history, Dad," said Ziva in a matter-of-fact tone. "So, where exactly are we going?"

"Just wait and see," answered Sholom Rabinowitz.

They found parking outside the walls and entered through the Jaffa Gate. Ziva's father led them downhill through the *souk*, the open-air market. They turned left and proceeded into the Muslim Quarter.

"I assume you all know," said Sholom, "that over a hundred years ago, Jews lived everywhere, in every quarter of the city."

"Yes," said Ori.

Eventually, they stood in front of an ancient building deep in the Muslim Quarter on El-Bustami Street. Sholom opened the door and led them through a short, dark passageway into a central courtyard. They all looked around at the three stories of balconies that surrounded the courtyard.

A door opened and a young Arab, dressed just like them, approached them.

"Can I help you?" he asked politely in Arabic-accented Hebrew.

"Yes, please," said Ziva's Dad. "We are looking for the Salman family."

"I am Mahmoud Salman. However, I think you want to see my grandfather, correct?" came the reply. "Please come with me."

Mahmoud led them across the courtyard and into one of the apartments. They entered a good-sized room with woven carpets on the floor and oversized pillows against the wall. In one corner sat a very old man. As they entered an old woman came into the room from inside the house. Mahmoud translated his grandfather's request to bring them coffee.

Grandfather Salman motioned for them to sit down—on the carpets—which they did. "I have been waiting for you to come for over seventy years," he said.

The Rabinowitzes and Yityish sat there stunned.

With Mahmoud translating into Hebrew, the grandfather told the following story, "When I was a young boy, my father gave me a large key to an empty apartment on the top floor. He told me that this was the apartment of the Rabinowitz family. When they moved away, they paid my father a great sum of money to guard the apartment. 'Do not let anyone inside,' my father instructed me.

Shopping in the outdoor marketplace, or souk, in the Muslim Quarter of the Old City, Jerusalem.

'Some day the Rabinowitzes will come back. You will give them the key.' So, now you have returned."

Mrs. Salman entered carrying a tray with small cups of coffee. "Our tradition," said Mahmoud, "Is to greet honored guests with hot, bitter coffee. This is an ancient tradition.[1] Our family also has a new tradition: Before you leave, we will serve you sweet coffee, so you will take with you the sweetness of your visit in our home."

As they sipped their coffee, Mahmoud continued, "I realize that many among our Palestinian people are your enemies. I know that our peoples have fought with each other and we are still trying to make peace with each other. However, here in our home, we honor our tradition and culture. Here, you are safe and we do not allow bad feelings to come between us."

Sholom Rabinowitz said thank you to Mahmoud and then turned to the grandfather and asked in fluent Arabic, "Have you ever been inside the Rabinowitz apartment?"

"Yes," replied the old man, "but only to clean it."

"Thank you," said Sholom. All of the young people, including Mahmoud, were surprised that Sholom spoke Arabic.

Mahmoud's grandfather got up and left the room to look for the key to the Rabinowitz apartment.

After an awkward moment of silence, Ziva said to Mahmoud, "You can see that we are each very different from one another, even though most of us are cousins. For the past two weeks, we have been learning how each of our families is different and unique. Can you tell us about your family and traditions?"

Mahmoud smiled. "Of course! First, you must know that my parents and my brothers and sisters do not live here with my grandfather. We live in a large house in East Jerusalem. My father is a lawyer and my mother is a teacher. Together with my cousins, the high-school-age grandchildren take turns spending the afternoon with my grandparents."

"Do you have a large family?" asked Nadav.

"Yes," answered Mahmoud. "I can see that your family has many kinds of people and so does mine. I have older cousins who are university graduates, while some of my cousins are involved in Israeli politics, working with different Israeli Arab Knesset (parliament) members. My mother has relatives who are shopkeepers and some of my father's relatives still live in villages and are farmers."[2]

After pausing, Mahmoud asked a question. "Do you know how many Israeli citizens are Arabs?"

The Rabinowitzes and Yityish answered, "No."

"I have studied Arab-Israeli history in school," continued Mahmoud proudly. "As I recall, there are about 1.7 million Arabs, and most of them are Muslim. Over half of them live in the northern part of Israel, just like my father's relatives. There are over 250,000 Bedouin Arabs. Traditionally, they were shepherds, and they moved around the land without permanent homes. Today, however, most of them have settled in the Negev, the southern section of the country. The Bedouins are also Muslim."[3]

"Aren't there other kinds of Arabs in Israel?" asked Ori.

"Yes," said Mahmoud. "There are the Christian Arabs and the Druze, each group with more than 120,000 citizens.[4] The Druze faith, which was based on Islam, is the newest of all the major religions in Israel. It was formed about one thousand years ago."[5]

Yityish added thoughtfully, "Many of the Arab women I see wear different kinds of clothing, but the men dress like everyone else."

"The Quran—our bible, so to speak—instructs all Muslims to dress modestly,"[6] responded Mahmoud. "As a result, many women, like my mother, dress like modern women, except they cover their heads with a *hijab*. More traditional women, like my grandmother, also wear a long, flowing dress, often with a cloak or robe over it. The traditional men like my grandfather wear a *thobe*, a long robe, with a *kuffiyeh* head scarf, which is held in place with a rope called an *egal*."[7]

Now it was Shmulik's turn to ask a question. "Am I correct in assuming that the *falafel*, *hummus*, and *tahina* that we Jewish Israelis love to eat are really Arab foods?"[8]

"Yes," answered Mahmoud. "But I'll tell you a secret. I really like pizza!"

Everyone laughed. As if on cue, Grandfather Salman entered the room. He said, "Please come with me."

After climbing two flights of stairs, they arrived outside a door, which Grandfather Salman unlocked. He then handed the key to Sholom, nodded his head, and proceeded down the stairs.

They discovered that the apartment had a sitting room, two bedrooms, and a small kitchen.

"Where's the bathroom?" asked Ori.

"Probably downstairs," replied Ziva's father.

Together, they explored the rooms, opening drawers and closets. Not much was there, only some very old pots, pans, and silverware. Everyone's face showed disappointment, except for Shmulik.

"This is fantastic!" he exclaimed.

"Why?" they asked all together.

"We are in the apartment of our great-great-great-grandparents. This is where the Rabinowitz family history in Israel begins," he said.

Young Arab Israeli girls offer prayer books to passing cars in the main street of Taybeh, Israel, in 2014.

"He's right," said Nadav.

"Hey, guys!" shouted Ori excitedly as he came in from a bedroom. "Look! I found a small box of photographs!"

They all gathered around Ori and one by one carefully looked at the photographs. There were Moshe and Hanna Rabinowitz. In some of the photos, they saw their great-great-grandfathers, Sholom, Isaac, and David. Now, everyone was excited.

"Just wait until everyone sees these photos!" said Shmulik.

"I have an idea," said Ziva as they locked up the apartment and went down the stairs to say thank you to the Salmans and to drink sweet coffee. "Let's have a big family get-together with everyone!"

"Great!" "Yes!" "Good!" they all exclaimed.

"Including my family?" asked Yityish.

"Yes!" they answered together.

51

The Western Wall

Over two thousand years ago, King Herod decided to repair the Second Temple in Jerusalem. He expanded the area surrounding the Temple, making it into a large plateau, called the Temple Mount. To support this expanded hilltop, he built very thick walls around it for support.[9]

When the Romans destroyed the Temple in 70 CE, they did not tear down the Temple Mount. As a result, parts of those walls are visible today. Since there are religious rules that forbid Jews from going up to the Temple Mount, a 187-foot exposed section of the western wall has

become a gathering place for Jews throughout the centuries. Hundreds of years before the Six-Day War in which the Israeli army recaptured the Temple Mount and the Western Wall, Jews came there to pray. Nowadays, the plaza in front of the Western Wall is filled with Jews, especially on the Sabbath and holidays.

One unique custom is to write a personal request on a slip of paper and to put it into one of the many cracks between the Western Wall's giant stones. Thus, a person's special request of God will remain there even after they have left.[10]

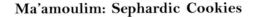

Experiencing Israeli Culture in the United States

Even if you don't live in Israel, there are many ways to experience Israeli culture in the United States. There may be an Israeli restaurant in your neighborhood that you can try. You could also rent an Israeli film. Listen to Israeli radio online (try a site like tunein.com), or take an Israeli dance class. Many dance studios offer Israeli dance, and Jewish Community Centers (JCCs) often teach this type of dance as well. You can also try your hand at the recipe and craft without even leaving your home!

Ma'amoulim: Sephardic Cookies

**Make this recipe with adult supervision.
Makes about 70 cookies.**

Ingredients

Dough:
4 cups of flour
2 cups of fine flour (semolina)
2 cups of margarine
1 cup of water
½ cup of sugar
¼ teaspoon of vanilla extract

Filling:
24 oz. of dates (dates may not be available at all supermarkets; try specialty grocers or natural food markets)
1 cup of chopped mixed nuts
1 teaspoon of cinnamon

Powdered sugar to
sprinkle on cookies

Instructions

1. Dough: Mix flour and semolina together in a bowl. In another bowl, mix together the remaining dough ingredients. Slowly add the flour mixture. Knead well. Make 70 small balls of dough. Place them on baking paper and let them "rest" for 30 minutes.

2. Filling: Remove the pits of the dates, and the cap on the end (if it's there). Slice the dates into quarters. Place the date pieces in a food processor and blend until smooth. Mix the date spread, nuts, and cinnamon together thoroughly for the filling.

3. After the dough has rested for 30 minutes, use a rolling pin to flatten each dough ball.

4. Take a teaspoon-full of the filling and spread it on one edge of the flattened dough ball. Fold the dough ball closed and seal the edges.

5. Place the cookies on a baking sheet on a flat baking pan. The dough does not rise, so the cookies can be placed right next to each other on the baking sheet.

6. Take a fork and gently score the top of each rolled cookie.

7. Bake in a preheated oven at 350°F for 20 minutes until lightly golden.

8. Remove from the oven and allow to cool.

9. Dust with powdered sugar and serve.

Facing Toward Jerusalem

For over two thousand years, Jews have prayed toward Jerusalem. Therefore, the direction depends on where a person is praying. For instance, in northern Israel, people pray facing south. In southern Israel, people pray facing north. To help them remember which way to face, Jews make colorful representations of Jerusalem and then hang them on the wall indicating the direction that they should face.

Here is how you can make your own design indicating the direction to Jerusalem. **Work on this project with adult supervision.**

Instructions

1. Start by gathering the materials and tools: colorful paper, a pair of scissors, and white glue.

2. Next, you need a design. See the picture below for an example of a stylized skyline of Jerusalem's Old City. You can make your own design by searching the Internet for pictures of Jerusalem.

3. Carefully cut out the pieces of colored paper in the shapes necessary to create your picture. Remember to cut out the shapes that are in the background first, then the shapes in the middle and lastly, the shapes in the foreground.

4. First, paste the background shapes on a sheet of white paper, then paste the shapes in the middle, and finally paste the shapes that are in front.

5. It is not necessary to follow the design exactly. Be creative. For instance, our original design is in black and white. So we chose the colors that we thought would look good. We added a blue paper for the sky and cut out a cloud. That left us space to write the word Jerusalem on top.

Map of Israel

CHAPTER NOTES

Introduction

1. Catherine Soanes and Angus Stevenson, eds., *Concise Oxford English Dictionary* (Oxford, NY: Oxford University Press, 2004), p. 349.
2. Dan Bahat, ed., *The Forgotten Generations* (Jerusalem: The Israel Economist, 1975).
3. State of Israel Ministry of Aliyah and Immigrant Absorption, "The First Aliyah (1882–1903)." http://www.moia.gov.il/English/FeelingIsrael/AboutIsrael/Pages/aliya1.aspx
4. H.H. Ben-Sasson, ed., *A History of the Jewish People* (Cambridge, MA: Harvard University Press, 1976), pp. 886, 921.
5. Ibid., pp. 1010, 1065.
6. Fred M. Gottheil, *Middle East Quarterly*, "The Smoking Gun: Arab Immigration into Palestine, 1922–1931," Winter 2003, pp. 53–64. http://www.meforum.org/522/the-smoking-gun-arab-immigration-into-palestine
7. Aviya Kushner, MyJewishLearning.com, "Israel's Vibrant Jewish Ethnic Mix." http://myjewishlearning.com/israel/Contemporary_Life/Society_and_Religious_Issues/Ashkenazic-Sephardic_Ethnic_Division.shtml?p=0
8. Aviad Klinger, Israel Central Bureau of Statistics, Demographics Sector, "65th Independence Day—More Than 8 Million Residents in the State of Israel," April 14, 2013. http://www1.cbs.gov.il/www/hodaot2013n/11_13_097e.pdf
9. ilMuseums. http://www.ilmuseums.com/
10. Israel Ministry of Tourism, "Arts in Israel." http://www.goisrael.com/Tourism_Eng/Tourist%20Information/Discover%20Israel/Pages/Arts.aspx
11. Hebrew Book Week. http://www.sfarim.org.il/

Chapter 1: A Strange Meeting

1. Israel Broadcasting Association. http://www.iba.org.il/
2. Israel Ministry of Tourism, "Arts in Israel." http://www.goisrael.com/tourism_eng/tourist%20information/discover%20israel/pages/arts.aspx#Paragraph4
3. Noa Fink-Shamit, The National Library of Israel, "Israeli Book Statistics for 2010." http://www.jnul.huji.ac.il/eng/lgd-statistics-2011.html

4. Go Jerusalem, "National Hebrew Book Week at 05.06.2013." http://www.gojerusalem.com/events/2065/National-Hebrew-Book-Week/
5. GlobalFirePower.com, "Countries Ranked by Military Strength (2014)," February 13, 2014. http://www.globalfirepower.com/countries-listing.asp
6. Israel Defense Forces. http://www.idf.il/english/
7 Israel Defense Forces, "History of the IDF." http://www.idf.il/1503-en/Dover.aspx

Chatper 2: Nadav

1. H.H. Ben-Sasson, ed., *A History of the Jewish People* (Cambridge, MA: Harvard University Press, 1976), p. 919.
2. Ibid., p. 1045.
3. Anita Shapira, ed., *Independence: The First Fifty Years* [Hebrew] (Jerusalem: Zalman Shazar Center for Jewish History, 1998), pp. 527–540.
4. American Overseas Dietetic Association, The Israeli Nutrition Week, "Israeli Eating Patterns." http://www.israelnutritionweek.com/israeli_nutrition.aspx
5. Dan Urian and Efraim Karsh, eds., *In Search of Identity: Jewish Aspects in Israeli Culture* (London: Frank Cass and Co., 1999), p. 132 ff.
6. Kibbutz Industries Association, "Commemorating 100 Years of the Kibbutz." http://www.kia.co.il/infoeng/kibbutz.htm

Chapter 3: Shmulik

1. Joan Nathan, *The Foods of Israel Today* (New York: Alfred A. Knopf, 2001), p. 322.
2. Mark Zborowski and Elizabeth Herzog, *Life is with People: The Culture of the Shtetl* (New York: Schocken Books, 1962), pp. 97–100.
3. Center for Educational Technology, "Yeshivot in Israel." http://lexicon.cet.ac.il/wf/wfTerm.aspx?id=1278

Chapter 4: Ori

1. Donna Rosenthal, *The Israelis: Ordinary People in an Extraordinary Land* (New York: Free Press, 2003), p. 119.
2. Ibid., p. 118.
3. Daniel J. Elazar, Jerusalem Center for Public Affairs, "How Religious are Israeli Jews?" http://www.jcpa.org/dje/articles2/howrelisr.htm

CHAPTER NOTES

4. Kevjn Lim, "From Plowshares to Swords: The Sephardi-Ashkenazi Schism and the Problems of Ethnic Discourse in Israel," November 2004. http://www.kevjnlim.com/other-research/from-plowshares-to-swords-the-sephardi-ashkenazi-schism-and-the-problems-of-ethnic-discourse-in-israel/
5. Ibid.
6. Donna Rosenthal, *The Israelis: Ordinary People in an Extraordinary Land* (New York: Free Press, 2003), p. 122.
7. Ibid., p. 118.
8. H.H. Ben-Sasson, ed., *A History of the Jewish People* (Cambridge, MA: Harvard University Press, 1976), p. 588–590.

Chapter 5: Ziva
1. H.H. Ben-Sasson, ed., *A History of the Jewish People* (Cambridge, MA: Harvard University Press, 1976), p. 1082–1089.
2. Anita Shapira, *Israeli Identity in Transition* (Wesport, CN: Praeger, 2004), pp. 223–228.
3. Israel Central Bureau of Statistics, *Immigration to Israel in 2012*, "Table 2—Immigrants, by Continent and Selected Last Country of Residence." http://www1.cbs.gov.il/hodaot2013n/21_13_050t2.pdf
4. Arnold Dashefsky, Sergio DellaPergola, and Ira Sheskin, eds., Berman Institute—North American Jewish Data Bank, "World Jewish Population, 2012," http://www.jewishdatabank.org/Studies/downloadFile.cfm?FileID=2941
5. Israel Ministry of Foreign Affairs, "The Long Road Home." http://mfa.gov.il/MFA/AboutIsrael/People/Pages/SOCIETY-%20Jewish%20Society.asp

Chapter 6: Yityish
1. Donna Rosenthal, *The Israelis: Ordinary People in an Extraordinary Land* (New York: Free Press, 2003), p. 158.
2. Ibid., p. 149.
3. Ibid.
4. Jewish Federations of North America, "The UJC Ethiopia Fact-Finding Report," October 29, 2000. http://www.jewishfederations.org/page.aspx?ID=797
5. Donna Rosenthal, *The Israelis: Ordinary People in an Extraordinary Land* (New York: Free Press, 2008), p. 171.
6. Ibid., p. 156.

7. Associated Press, *Haaretz*, "Israel Putting End to Millenia-Old Tradition of Ethiopian Jewish Priests," January 18, 2012. http://www.haaretz.com/jewish-world/israel-putting-end-to-millenia-old-tradition-of-ethiopian-jewish-priests-1.407958
8. Donna Rosenthal, *The Israelis: Ordinary People in an Extraordinary Land* (New York: Free Press, 2003), p. 163.
9. Knesset, "Sigd—A Holiday of Ethiopian Jewry." http://www.knesset.gov.il/lexicon/eng/sigd_eng.htm
10. Rebecca L. Torstrick, *Culture and Customs of Israel* (Westport, CT: Greenwood Press, 2004), p. 109.

Chapter 7: Mahmoud
1. Asmaa Al-Ghoul, translated by Tyler Huffman, *Al-Monitor*, "Coffee in Gaza is a Ritual for Grief and Creativity," January 17, 2014. http://www.al-monitor.com/pulse/originals/2014/01/coffee-gaza-rituals-tradition-grief.html#
2. Israel Ministry of Foreign Affairs, "People: Minority Communities." http://mfa.gov.il/MFA/AboutIsrael/People/Pages/SOCIETY-%20Minority%20Communities.aspx
3. Ibid.
4. Ibid.
5. Druze Heritage Foundation, "The Druze Faith: Introduction." http://druzeheritage.org/DHF/The_Druze_Faith.asp
6. Christine Huda Dodge, "Islamic Clothing Requirements." http://islam.about.com/od/dress/p/clothing_reqs.htm
7. Christine Huda Dodge, "Islamic Clothing Glossary." http://islam.about.com/od/dress/tp/clothing-glossary.htm
8. Julian Kossoff, *The Telegraph*, "The Arab-Israeli Conflict Turns into a Food Fight," March 18, 2011. http://blogs.telegraph.co.uk/news/juliankossoff/100079665/the-arab-israeli-conflict-turns-into-a-food-fight/
9. Go Jerusalem, "King Herod: Tyrant and Builder." http://www.gojerusalem.com/article/300/King-Herod%3A-Tyrant-and-Builder----/
10. Julie Stahl, CBN News, "What Happens to Prayers at the Western Wall?" June 8, 2012. http://www.cbn.com/cbnnews/insideisrael/2012/May/What-Happens-to-Prayers-at-the-Western-Wall/

FURTHER READING

Books

Abbey, Alan D. *Journey of Hope: the Story of Ilan Ramon, Israel's First Astronaut.* Jerusalem: Gefen Publishing House, 2003.

Bamberger, David. *A Young Person's History of Israel.* West Orange, NJ: Behrman House, 1995.

Schroeter, Daniel J. *Israel: An Illustrated History.* New York: Oxford University Press, 1998.

Sherman, Josepha. *Your Travel Guide to Ancient Israel.* Minneapolis, MN: Lerner Publications, 2004.

Slavicek, Louise Chipley. *Creation of the Modern Middle East: Israel.* New York: Chelsea House Publishers, 2008.

Smith, Debbie. *Israel: the Culture.* New York: Crabtree Pub. Co., 2007.

Sofer, Barbara. *Kids Love Israel, Israel Loves Kids: A Travel Guide for Families.* Rockville, MD: Kar-Ben Copies, 1996.

On the Internet

Falasha! The Saga of Ethiopian Jewry
Part 1 http://www.youtube.com/watch?v=C5QNOq_EWhc
Part 2 http://www.youtube.com/watch?v=lRIjqFwOrME

Judaism 101: Ashkenazic and Sephardic Jews
http://www.jewfaq.org/ashkseph.htm

National Geographic Kids: Israel
http://kids.nationalgeographic.com/kids/places/find/israel/

Time for Kids: *Around the World,* "Israel"
http://www.timeforkids.com/destination/israel

Works Consulted

American Overseas Dietetic Association. "Israeli Eating Patterns." The Israeli Nutrition Week. http://www.israelnutritionweek.com/israeli_nutrition.aspx

Associated Press. "Israel Putting End to Millenia-Old Tradition of Ethiopian Jewish Priests." *Haaretz,* January 18, 2012. http://www.haaretz.com/jewish-world/israel-putting-end-to-millenia-old-tradition-of-ethiopian-jewish-priests-1.407958

Bahat, Dan, ed. *The Forgotten Generations.* Jerusalem: The Israel Economist, 1975.

Ben-Sasson, H.H., ed. *A History of the Jewish People.* Cambridge, MA: Harvard University Press, 1976.

Biale, David, ed. *Cultures of the Jews: A New History.* New York: Schocken Books, 2002.

Center for Educational Technology. "Yeshivot in Israel." http://lexicon.cet.ac.il/wf/wfTerm.aspx?id=1278

Cohen, Asher, and Bernard Susser. *Israel and the Politics of Jewish Identity.* Baltimore, MD: The Johns Hopkins University Press, 2000.

Dashefsky, Arnold, Sergio DellaPergola, and Ira Sheskin, eds. "World Jewish Population, 2012." Berman Institute—North American Jewish Data Bank. http://www.jewishdatabank.org/Studies/downloadFile.cfm?FileID=2941

Dodge, Christine Huda. "Islamic Clothing Glossary." http://islam.about.com/od/dress/tp/clothing-glossary.htm

Dodge, Christine Huda. "Islamic Clothing Requirements." http://islam.about.com/od/dress/p/clothing_reqs.htm

Druze Heritage Foundation. "The Druze Faith: Introduction." http://druzeheritage.org/DHF/The_Druze_Faith.asp

Elazar, Daniel J. "How Religious are Israeli Jews?" Jerusalem Center for Public Affairs. http://www.jcpa.org/dje/articles2/howrelisr.htm

Elon, Amos. *Jerusalem: City of Mirrors.* London: Fontana, 1991.

Fink-Shamit, Noa. "Israeli Book Statistics for 2010." The National Library of Israel. http://www.jnul.huji.ac.il/eng/lgd-statistics-2011.html

Gavron, Daniel. *The Kibbutz: Awakening from Utopia.* Lanham, MD: Rowman & Littlefield Publishers, 2000.

Al-Ghoul, Asmaa. Translated by Tyler Huffman. "Coffee in Gaza is a Ritual for Grief and Creativity." *Al-Monitor,* January 17, 2014. http://www.al-monitor.com/pulse/originals/2014/01/coffee-gaza-rituals-tradition-greif.html#

GlobalFirePower.com. "Countries Ranked by Military Strength (2014)." February 13, 2014. http://www.globalfirepower.com/countries-listing.asp

Go Jerusalem. "King Herod: Tyrant and Builder." http://www.gojerusalem.com/article/300/King-Herod%3A-Tyrant-and-Builder----/

Go Jerusalem. "National Hebrew Book Week at 05.06.2013." http://www.gojerusalem.com/events/2065/National-Hebrew-Book-Week/

Goldscheider, Calvin. *Israel's Changing Society: Population, Ethnicity, & Development.* Boulder, CO: Westview Press, 1996.

Gottheil, Fred M. "The Smoking Gun: Arab Immigration into Palestine, 1922-1931." *Middle East Quarterly,* Winter 2003, pp. 53-64. http://www.meforum.org/522/the-smoking-gun-arab-immigration-into-palestine

Haïk, Daniel. "Ashkenazim, Sephardim: Time for Self Scrutiny." i24News, August 13, 2013. http://www.i24news.tv/en/opinion/130813-ashkenazim-it-s-time-for-self-scrutiny

Hebrew Book Week. http://www.sfarim.org.il/

Hertzog, Esther. *Immigrants & Bureaucrats: Ethiopians in an Israeli Absorption Center.* New York: Berghahn Books, 1999.

Herzog, Hanna, Tal Kohavi, Shimshon Zelniker, eds., *Generations, Locations, Identities: Contemporary Perspectives on Society and Culture in Israel* [Hebrew]. Jerusalem: Van Leer Institute and HaKibbutz Hameuchad, 2007.

Hillel Shulewitz, Malka, ed. *The Forgotten Millions: The Modern Jewish Exodus from Arab Lands.* London: Cassell, 1999.

ilMuseums. http://www.ilmuseums.com/

Israel Broadcasting Association. http://www.iba.org.il/

FURTHER READING

Israel Central Bureau of Statistics. *Immigration to Israel in 2012.* "Table 2—Immigrants, by Continent and Selected Last Country of Residence." http://www1.cbs.gov.il/hodaot2013n/21_13_050t2.pdf

Israel Defense Forces. http://www.idf.il/english/

Israel Defense Forces. "History of the IDF." http://www.idf.il/1503-en/Dover.aspx

Israel Ministry of Foreign Affairs. "People: Minority Communities." http://mfa.gov.il/MFA/AboutIsrael/People/Pages/SOCIETY-%20Minority%20Communities.aspx

Israel Ministry of Foreign Affairs. "The Long Road Home." http://mfa.gov.il/MFA/AboutIsrael/People/Pages/SOCIETY-%20Jewish%20Society.aspx

Israel Ministry of Tourism. "Arts in Israel." http://www.goisrael.com/tourism_eng/tourist%20information/discover%20israel/pages/arts.aspx#Paragraph4

Jewish Agency for Israel. "Israel and Zionism—Highlights." http://jafi.org/JewishAgency/English/Jewish+Education/Compelling+Content/Eye+on+Israel

Jewish Federations of North America. "The UJC Ethiopia Fact-Finding Report." October 29, 2000. http://www.jewishfederations.org/page.aspx?ID=797

Katriel, Tamar. *Communal Webs: Communication and Culture in Contemporary Israel.* Albany: State University of New York Press, 1991.

Kibbutz Industries Association. "Commemorating 100 Years of the Kibbutz." http://www.kia.co.il/infoeng/kibbutz.htm

Klinger, Aviad. "65th Independence Day—More Than 8 Million Residents in the State of Israel." Israel Central Bureau of Statistics, Demographics Sector, April 14, 2013. http://www1.cbs.gov.il/www/hodaot2013n/11_13_097e.pdf

Knesset. "Sigd—A Holiday of Ethiopian Jewry." http://www.knesset.gov.il/lexicon/eng/sigd_eng.htm

Kossoff, Julian. "The Arab-Israeli Conflict Turns into a Food Fight." *The Telegraph*, March 18, 2011. http://blogs.telegraph.co.uk/news/juliankossoff/100079665/the-arab-israeli-conflict-turns-into-a-food-fight/

Kushner, Aviya. "Israel's Vibrant Jewish Ethnic Mix." MyJewishLearning.com. http://myjewishlearning.com/israel/Contemporary_Life/Society_and_Religious_Issues/Ashkenazic-Sephardic_Ethnic_Division.shtml?p=0

Liebman, Charles S. *Reconceptualizing the Culture Conflict among Israeli Jews.* Ramat Gan: Jolson Center for Israel, Judaism & Democracy, Bar Ilan University, 2001.

Lim, Kevjn. "From Plowshares to Swords: The Sephardi-Ashkenazi Schism and the Problems of Ethnic Discourse in Israel." November 2004. http://www.kevjnlim.com/other-research/from-plowshares-to-swords-the-sephardi-ashkenazi-schism-and-the-problems-of-ethnic-discourse-in-israel/

———. "The Haredi-Secular Schism: Engaging the Ultra-Orthodox in Israeli Polity and Society." September 2004. http://www.kevjnlim.com/other-research/the-haredi-secular-schism-engaging-the-ultra-orthodox-in-israeli-polity-and-society/

Lyons, Len. *The Ethiopian Jews of Israel.* Woodstock, VT: Jewish Lights Publishing, 2007.

MyJewishLearning.com. "Israeli Society & Religious Issues." http://www.myjewishlearning.com/israel/Contemporary_Life/Society_and_Religious_Issues.shtml?p=1

Nathan, Joan. *The Foods of Israel Today.* New York: Alfred A. Knopf, 2001.

Rosenthal, Donna. *Passport Israel: Your Pocket Guide to Israeli Business, Customs & Etiquette.* San Rafael, CA: World Trade Press, 1997.

Rosenthal, Donna. *The Israelis: Ordinary People in an Extraordinary Land.* New York: Free Press, 2003 and 2008.

Seeman, Don. *One People, One Blood: Ethiopian-Israelis and the Return to Judaism.* New Brunswick, NJ: Rutgers University Press, 2009.

Segev, Tom. *Elvis in Jerusalem: Post-Zionism and the Americanization of Israel.* New York: Metropolitan Books, 2002.

Shapira, Anita, ed. *Independence: The First Fifty Years* [Hebrew]. Jerusalem: Zalman Shazar Center for Jewish History, 1998.

———. *Israeli Identity in Transition.* Wesport, CT: Praeger, 2004.

Shasha, David. "Masking Identity: Sephardim as Ashkenazim." Hakeshet Hademocratit Hamizrahit. http://www.ha-keshet.org.il/english/Masking.htm

Soanes, Catherine, and Angus Stevenson, eds. *Concise Oxford English Dictionary.* Oxford, NY: Oxford University Press, 2004.

Stahl, Julie. "What Happens to Prayers at the Western Wall?" CBN News, June 8, 2012. http://www.cbn.com/cbnnews/insideisrael/2012/May/What-Happens-to-Prayers-at-the-Western-Wall/

State of Israel Ministry of Aliyah and Immigrant Absorption. "The First Aliyah (1882-1903)." http://www.moia.gov.il/English/FeelingIsrael/AboutIsrael/Pages/aliya1.aspx

Torstrick, Rebecca L. *Culture and Customs of Israel.* Westport, CT: Greenwood Press, 2004.

Urian, Dan, and Karsh Efraim, eds. *In Search of Identity: Jewish Aspects in Israeli Culture.* London: Frank Cass and Co., 1999.

Van Creveld, Martin. *The Sword and the Olive: A Critical History of the Israeli Defense Force.* New York: PublicAffairs, 2002.

Winter, Dick. *Culture Shock! A Guide to Customs and Etiquette—Israel.* London: Kuperard, 1992.

Zborowski, Mark, and Elizabeth Herzog. *Life is with People: The Culture of the Shtetl.* New York: Schocken Books, 1962.

GLOSSARY

aliyah (ah-lee-AH)—A Hebrew word meaning to go up, it refers to the immigration of the Jews to the land of Israel.

anti-Semitism (an-tee-SEM-ih-tiz-uhm)—Discrimination against or negative feelings towards Jews.

Ashkenazic Jews (ahsh-kuh-NAH-zik)—Jews of central and eastern European origin or ancestry.

commandments (com-MAND-muhnts)—According to the Jewish religion, God commanded the Jews to observe 613 laws, asking them to do such things as observe the Jewish holidays, while forbidding them to do other things, including robbery and murder.

dialect (DAHY-uh-lekt)—A distinct way of speaking a language.

exile (EK-sahyl)—To send a person away from his or her country and forbid that person to return.

falafel (fuh-LAH-fuhl)—Fried balls of ground chickpeas and spices that are often eaten in a pita with chopped tomatoes and cucumbers.

haredi (ha-RAY-dee, singular) **haredim** (ha-RAY-deem, plural)—Strictly religious Jews.

Hebrew (HEE-broo)—The language of the Bible and of modern Israel.

Holocaust (HOL-uh-kawst)—The attempt by Nazi Germany to murder the entire Jewish people during World War II.

IDF—Initials that stand for Israel Defense Forces, the name of the Israeli armed forces.

kibbutz (ki-BOOTS)—A rural Israeli community where the member families share facilities and property.

kippah (KEE-pah)—A cap worn by religious Jewish men, which can be made of different materials, including colorful knitted thread.

kosher (KOH-sher)—The Hebrew word meaning fit for use, which is most commonly used for food that meets the requirements of Jewish laws and customs.

nationalist (NASH-uh-nl-ist)—A person devoted to his or her nation.

Ottoman (OT-uh-mun)—Refers to the Ottoman Empire that was centered in modern-day Turkey.

Passover (PAHS-oh-ver)—The Jewish holiday celebrating the exodus (leaving) of the Jews from slavery in Egypt in Biblical times.

persecution (pur-si-KYOO-shuhn)—A program to kill or harm people because of their religion, race, or beliefs.

pogrom (puh-GROM)—A riot led by anti-Semites for the purpose of murdering Jews and destroying their property.

rabbi (RAB-ahy)—A Jewish religious leader.

Rosh Hashanah (ROHSH hah-SHAW-nuh or hah-shah-NAH)—A two-day holiday at the beginning of the seventh month on the Jewish calendar, which marks the Jewish New Year. It is celebrated with the sounding of a ram's horn.

Sabbath (SAB-uhth)—The seventh day of the week; the Jewish Sabbath always occurs on Saturday. It is a day of rest devoted to prayer, study, and family.

secular (SEK-yuh-ler)—Referring to worldly things other than religion or to a person who is not religious.

seder (SEY-der)—The festival meal on the first night of Passover.

Sephardic Jew (suh-FAHR-dik)—A Jew whose origins can be traced to Spain or Portugal in the 1400s.

sidelocks—Long, often curled hair that grows next to the ears. Many very religious Jewish men wear sidelocks.

socialist (SOH-shuh-list)—A person who believes in socialism, the idea that all wealth should be shared.

synagogue (SIN-uh-gog)—A Jewish place of worship.

Temple in Jerusalem—The Jewish people built two giant Temples in Jerusalem. The Temple was the center of Jewish worship. The first was destroyed by the Babylonians in 586 BCE. The second Temple was destroyed by the Romans in 70 CE.

yeshiva (yuh-SHEE-vuh)—A Jewish religious school devoted to the study of Jewish religious texts and ideas.

Yom Kippur (yawm kee-POOR)—The tenth day of the seventh month on the Jewish calendar, Yom Kippur is a day of fasting and praying, asking God for forgiveness.

Zionist (ZAHY-un-nist)—A person who believes in the establishment of the State of Israel and the return of all of the world's Jews to Israel.

INDEX

About the Author

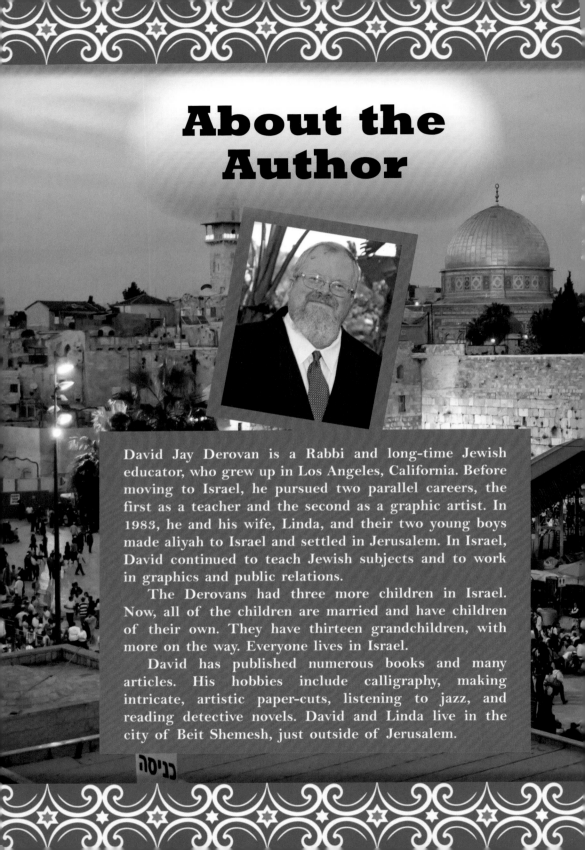

David Jay Derovan is a Rabbi and long-time Jewish educator, who grew up in Los Angeles, California. Before moving to Israel, he pursued two parallel careers, the first as a teacher and the second as a graphic artist. In 1983, he and his wife, Linda, and their two young boys made aliyah to Israel and settled in Jerusalem. In Israel, David continued to teach Jewish subjects and to work in graphics and public relations.

The Derovans had three more children in Israel. Now, all of the children are married and have children of their own. They have thirteen grandchildren, with more on the way. Everyone lives in Israel.

David has published numerous books and many articles. His hobbies include calligraphy, making intricate, artistic paper-cuts, listening to jazz, and reading detective novels. David and Linda live in the city of Beit Shemesh, just outside of Jerusalem.

כניסה